CHRISTMAS GIFTS
from the KITCHEN

GEORGEANNE BRENNAN

CONTENTS

During the holidays, I spend more time in the kitchen than I do at any other time of the year, not only cooking for family and guests, but making cookies, candies, and savories to give as gifts. It is a special season that I treasure. I keep the fire in the kitchen fireplace glowing, and the gentle scent of wood smoke mingles with that of spiced wine and cider, of toasting walnuts and baking cookies throughout the day. The kitchen table is laden with decorative folding boxes for candy, cookies, and nuts; glass jars for pickles and jams; and boxes of ribbons, wrappings, and tags. Part of the fun of making gifts from the kitchen is in deciding how to present them and then carefully labeling "Lemon Zest Shortbread" on one gift tag or "Sugar and Spice Pecans" on another.

I hope that the recipes and ideas in this book will inspire you to create special gifts from your kitchen and enrich your holiday season as much as they do mine. Each year I eagerly anticipate the time when I will surround myself with the aromas of my kitchen as I prepare delicious, homemade gifts of holiday cheer for friends and family.

Georgeanne Brennan

COOKIES

Toasted Coconut Thumbprint Cookies

To toast the coconut for this recipe, spread it on a rimmed baking sheet and bake in a 325°F (165°C) oven, stirring once or twice, until golden, about 8 minutes.

✧ Preheat oven to 350°F (180°C). Have ready 2 ungreased baking sheets. Line the sheets with parchment (baking) paper, if desired.

✧ In a large bowl, using an electric mixer on medium speed, beat the butter, sugar, and salt until light and fluffy. Add the egg yolks and the vanilla and coconut extracts and beat until well blended. Reduce the mixer speed to low and gradually beat in the flour just until blended. Place the toasted coconut in a shallow bowl. In another bowl, lightly beat the egg whites.

✧ Using lightly floured hands, shape the dough into 1-inch (2.5-cm) balls. Dip each ball in the beaten whites and then roll evenly in the coconut, pressing to help it adhere. Arrange the balls on the baking sheets, spacing them about 1 inch apart. Press a fingertip into the center of each ball to make a small indentation (if the dough is sticky, coat your finger with flour). Spoon about ¼ teaspoon of the jam into each hollow.

✧ Bake the cookies until the tops look dry, 10–12 minutes. Let cool on the baking sheets on wire racks for 15 minutes. Transfer to the racks to cool completely.

1 cup (8 oz/250 g) unsalted butter, at room temperature

⅔ cup (5 oz/155 g) sugar

¼ teaspoon salt

2 large eggs, separated

1 teaspoon vanilla extract (essence)

¼ teaspoon coconut extract (essence)

2½ cups (12½ oz/390 g) all-purpose (plain) flour

2½ cups (10 oz/315 g) sweetened shredded dried coconut, toasted (see note)

About ¼ cup (2½ oz/75 g) apricot, raspberry, or strawberry jam

MAKES ABOUT 3 DOZEN COOKIES

Lemon Cookies with Wintry Decorations

These buttery cookies make perfect small canvases for colorful decorations. If you like, use a thin straw to punch a hole in the dough before baking, then attach a ribbon to the finished cookie to hang it as an ornament.

✧ Preheat oven to 350°F (180°C). Lightly grease 2 baking sheets or line them with parchment (baking) paper.

✧ In a large bowl, using an electric mixer on medium speed, beat the butter, granulated sugar, lemon zest, and salt until light and fluffy. Add the egg yolk and lemon juice and beat until blended. Reduce the mixer speed to low and gradually beat in the flour just until blended and the dough comes together.

✧ Turn out the dough onto a work surface. Divide the dough in half, gather up each portion, and press into a disk. Wrap 1 disk in plastic wrap and set aside. (If the dough is soft, wrap both disks and refrigerate until firm, about 30 minutes.)

✧ Place the unwrapped dough disk on a floured work surface and sprinkle with flour. Roll out the dough ¼ inch (6 mm) thick, sprinkling more flour under and over the dough as needed to prevent sticking.

✧ Using a 2½-inch (6-cm) cookie cutter, cut out as many cookies as possible, cutting them close together. Pull the scraps of dough from the shapes and set aside. Using an offset spatula, carefully transfer the cookies to the prepared baking sheets, spacing them about ¾ inch (2 cm) apart. Gather up the reserved dough scraps and gently press them into a disk. Repeat the rolling and cutting with the scraps and then with the second dough disk.

✧ Bake the cookies until lightly browned around the edges, about 12 minutes. Let cool on the baking sheets on wire racks for 5 minutes. Transfer to the racks to cool completely before decorating.

✧ To make the icing, in a large bowl, using the mixer on medium speed, combine the meringue powder and warm water. Reduce the mixer speed to low and beat in the confectioners' sugar until blended, then beat on high speed until thick and smooth,

about 5 minutes. Beat in more warm water, 1 tablespoon at a time, if the icing is too thick to spread or pipe. If coloring the icing, divide it among small bowls, one per color. Add a drop or so of coloring to each bowl and stir until blended, repeating as needed to create the desired color.

✧ Using a pastry bag fitted with a narrow tip, outline the edges of each cookie with icing, then use a small, damp pastry brush to spread an even layer of icing within the border. (If the icing is too thick, add a drop of warm water and stir until blended.) Or, use the pastry bag to pipe designs on the cookies. Let the icing set completely. While the icing is still soft, decorate the cookies with colored sugars, sprinkles, or other decorations. Let set completely.

1 cup (8 oz/250 g) unsalted butter, at room temperature

1 cup (8 oz/250 g) granulated sugar

1 teaspoon grated lemon zest

¼ teaspoon salt

1 large egg yolk

1 tablespoon fresh lemon juice

2¼ cups (11 oz/345 g) all-purpose (plain) flour

Royal Icing

3 tablespoons meringue powder

6 tablespoons (3 fl oz/90 ml) warm water, plus more if needed

4 cups (1 lb/500 g) confectioners' (icing) sugar, sifted

Assorted food colorings (optional)

Assorted colored decorating sugars, sprinkles, or other decorations

MAKES ABOUT 3 DOZEN COOKIES

Cookies as Gifts

ASSORTED CONTAINERS • RIBBON • RECIPE CARDS

1 Gather a mix of pretty containers, such as glass jars, old-fashioned tins, straw or wicker baskets, and wooden or paper boxes. Find some festive ribbon, either striped, sateen, silk, or raffia. Use heavy-weight paper for recipe cards and a colorful pen for writing.

2 Layer the cookies in each container, being careful to place more fragile confections on top. Include a combination of cookies or focus on one favorite.

3 Thread some ribbon through the recipe card and tie the card to the top of the container. If you like, add an extra holiday flourish, such as a sprig of pine or a small bell. You can also include multiple recipe cards.

Hazelnut Amaretti

The pearl sugar used to top these cookies is available at specialty-food stores, but coarsely crushed sugar cubes work well, too. Wrap each cookie in tissue paper, twist the ends, and pack in cookie tins.

✧ Preheat oven to 300°F (150°C). Line 2 baking sheets with parchment (baking) paper.

✧ In a food processor, finely grind the hazelnuts (do not grind to a paste). Add ¼ cup (1 oz/30 g) of the confectioners' sugar and grind to a powder. Mix in the remaining ½ cup (2 oz/60 g) plus 3 tablespoons confectioners' sugar and the flour.

✧ In a bowl, using an electric mixer on high speed, beat the egg whites until soft peaks form. Gradually add the granulated sugar and beat until stiff, shiny peaks form. Using a rubber spatula, fold in the almond extract and the hazelnut and sugar mixture.

✧ Spoon the batter into a pastry bag fitted with a ½-inch (12-mm) plain tip. Pipe the batter onto the prepared baking sheets in mounds 1½ inches (4 cm) in diameter, spacing them about 1 inch (2.5 cm) apart. Using a wet finger, smooth the top of each cookie. Sprinkle with pearl sugar, if desired.

✧ Bake the cookies until just beginning to brown, about 45 minutes. Turn off the oven, leave the oven door closed, and let the cookies dry for 30 minutes.

✧ Transfer the cookies to wire racks to cool completely. They will keep in an airtight container at room temperature for up to 1 month.

1¼ cups (6½ oz/200 g) hazelnuts (filberts)

¾ cup (3 oz/90 g) plus 3 tablespoons confectioners' (icing) sugar

1 teaspoon all-purpose (plain) flour

2 large egg whites

⅓ cup (3 oz/90 g) granulated sugar

¾ teaspoon almond extract (essence)

Pearl sugar for topping (optional)

MAKES ABOUT 3 DOZEN COOKIES

Toasted Pecan Butter Cookies

Pecans, which are native to North America and are cultivated primarily in the American South, are harvested in the fall, making them a popular ingredient in an array of holiday sweets.

1 cup (8 oz/250 g) unsalted butter, at room temperature

⅔ cup (5 oz/155 g) sugar

Pinch of salt

1 teaspoon vanilla extract (essence)

2¼ cups (11 oz/345 g) all-purpose (plain) flour

⅔ cup (3 oz/90 g) chopped pecans, toasted

MAKES ABOUT 3 DOZEN COOKIES

✧ In a large bowl, using an electric mixer on medium speed, beat the butter, sugar, and salt until light and fluffy. Add the vanilla and beat until well blended. Reduce the mixer speed to low and gradually beat in the flour and pecans just until blended.

✧ Turn out the dough onto a large sheet of plastic wrap. Use the plastic wrap to shape the dough into a log about 8 inches (20 cm) long and 2 inches (5 cm) in diameter. Wrap the log in a second sheet of plastic wrap and refrigerate until firm, about 3 hours.

✧ Preheat oven to 350°F (180°C). Line 2 baking sheets with parchment (baking) paper.

✧ Unwrap the chilled dough and, using a thin, sharp knife, cut the log into slices ¼ inch (6 mm) thick. Arrange the slices on the prepared baking sheets, spacing them 1 inch (2.5 cm) apart.

✧ Bake the cookies until golden brown around the edges, about 14 minutes. Let cool on the baking sheets on wire racks for 15 minutes. Transfer to the racks to cool completely.

Ginger Crisps

As they bake, these spice–laden cookies fill your kitchen with an irresistible aroma that evokes Christmas. Be sure to store them in an airtight container so that they remain crisp.

✧ In a bowl, combine the flour, ginger, cinnamon, nutmeg, baking soda, and salt. Stir until well blended. In a large bowl, using an electric mixer on medium speed, beat the butter and brown sugar until light and fluffy. Add the egg yolk and molasses and beat until well blended. Reduce the mixer speed to medium-low and gradually beat in the flour mixture until the dough is well blended and forms moist pebbles.

✧ Turn out the dough onto a lightly floured work surface. Knead gently until smooth. Shape the dough into a squared-off log 8 inches (20 cm) long. Wrap in plastic wrap and refrigerate until firm, about 3 hours.

✧ Preheat oven to 350°F (180°C). Line 2 baking sheets with parchment (baking) paper.

✧ Unwrap the chilled dough and, using a thin, sharp knife, cut the log into slices ¼ inch (6 mm) thick. Arrange the slices on the prepared baking sheets, spacing them 1 inch (2 cm) apart.

✧ Bake the cookies until slightly darker brown around the edges, about 10 minutes. Let cool on the baking sheets on wire racks for 15 minutes. Transfer to the racks to cool completely.

1⅔ cups (8½ oz/265 g) all-purpose (plain) flour

1 teaspoon ground ginger

¾ teaspoon ground cinnamon

Pinch of freshly grated nutmeg

½ teaspoon baking soda (bicarbonate of soda)

¼ teaspoon salt

½ cup (4 oz/125 g) unsalted butter, at room temperature

⅔ cup (5 oz/155 g) firmly packed brown sugar

1 large egg yolk

2 tablespoons unsulfured light molasses

MAKES ABOUT 3 DOZEN COOKIES

Orange-Oatmeal Lace Cookies

Easy to prepare and gorgeous to behold, these delicate lacy cookies are an elegant gift for cookie lovers. They are good for dessert or tea time and are always a hit at parties.

¾ cup (6 oz/185 g) sugar

¾ cup (2½ oz/75 g) quick-cooking oats

¾ cup (4 oz/125 g) all-purpose (plain) flour

½ teaspoon baking powder

½ cup (4 oz/125 g) plus 2 tablespoons unsalted butter, melted

¼ cup (2 fl oz/60 ml) whole milk

¼ cup (3 oz/90 g) unsulfured light molasses

1 tablespoon grated orange zest

1 teaspoon vanilla extract (essence)

Chocolate Coating

8 oz (250 g) semisweet (plain) or bittersweet chocolate, chopped

2 teaspoons vegetable shortening

MAKES ABOUT 4 DOZEN COOKIES

✧ Preheat oven to 350°F (180°C). Line 2 baking sheets with parchment (baking) paper.

✧ In a bowl, combine the sugar, oats, flour, and baking powder. Add the melted butter, milk, molasses, orange zest, and vanilla and stir until just blended. Let the batter stand for 15 minutes.

✧ Drop heaping tablespoonfuls of the batter onto the prepared baking sheets, forming rounds about 1 inch (2.5 cm) in diameter and spacing them 3 inches (7.5 cm) apart. Bake the cookies until brown on the edges, about 10 minutes. Lift the parchment paper with the cookies and transfer to a work surface. Let cool completely.

✧ Meanwhile, to make the Chocolate Coating: Combine the chocolate and shortening in the top pan of a double boiler or in a heatproof bowl. Set over (not touching) simmering water and stir until the chocolate is melted and smooth. Remove from the heat.

✧ Gently peel the cookies from the paper. Line the baking sheets again with parchment paper. Dip about half of each cooled cookie in the Chocolate Coating. Place on the prepared baking sheets. Refrigerate until the chocolate sets, about 20 minutes. Gently remove the cookies from the paper.

Coconut and Almond Macaroons

In this decadent version of a holiday favorite, chewy, nutty macaroons are dipped in rich bittersweet chocolate. Packed in even a simple box, these pretty treats make an impressive presentation.

3½ cups (10½ oz/330 g) sweetened, flaked coconut

1 cup (4 oz/125 g) sliced (flaked) almonds

½ cup (4 fl oz/125 ml) sweetened condensed milk

½ teaspoon almond extract (essence)

2 large egg whites

1 tablespoon sugar

Pinch of salt

Chocolate Coating (page 21)

MAKES ABOUT 1½ DOZEN COOKIES

✧ Preheat oven to 350°F (180°C). Line 2 baking sheets with parchment (baking) paper.

✧ In a baking pan, combine 1½ cups (4½ oz/140 g) of the coconut and the almonds. Toast, stirring occasionally, until golden, about 12 minutes. Transfer immediately to a bowl and let cool. Leave the oven on.

✧ In a bowl, combine the cooled coconut mixture, remaining coconut, condensed milk, and almond extract. In another bowl, using an electric mixer on high speed, beat the egg whites, sugar, and salt until soft peaks form. Using a rubber spatula, gently fold the egg whites into the coconut mixture.

✧ Using a large spoon, drop the dough into mounds about 2 inches (5 cm) in diameter on the prepared baking sheets, spacing them 2 inches apart. Bake the cookies until golden brown, about 10 minutes. Transfer to wire racks to cool completely.

✧ Line the 2 baking sheets again with parchment paper. Dip the bottoms of the cookies into the Chocolate Coating and transfer, chocolate side down, to the prepared baking sheets. Refrigerate the cookies until the chocolate is set.

Lemon Zest Shortbread

Crumbly, rich, and buttery shortbread is a classic treat with coffee or tea after a meal, and is also excellent with compotes, ice creams, or granita. Pack these cookies in pretty tins for an always-welcome gift.

✧ Preheat oven to 325°F (165°C).

✧ In a food processor, combine the flour, ⅓ cup granulated sugar, confectioners' sugar, lemon zest, and salt and process briefly to blend. Add the butter and process just until the mixture resembles coarse meal. Turn out the dough onto a floured work surface and gather it into a rough ball.

✧ Pat the dough evenly over the bottom of an ungreased 10-inch (25-cm) springform pan or tart pan with a removable bottom. Press the tines of a fork around the edge to form a decorative border and pierce the surface every 2 inches (5 cm) with the fork. Sprinkle with the 1 tablespoon granulated sugar. Or, to make individual cookies, turn out the dough onto a large sheet of plastic wrap and form into a log about 8 inches (20 cm) long. Wrap in plastic and refrigerate until firm. Cut into slices ¼ inch (6 mm) thick and arrange on an ungreased baking sheet, spacing them about 1 inch (2.5 cm) apart. Bake the cookies until the edges are golden, about 14 minutes.

✧ Bake the shortbread until the edges are lightly golden and the center is firm to the touch, 45–50 minutes. Let cool in the pan on a wire rack for 10 minutes.

✧ Carefully remove the sides of the pan. Using a long, sharp knife, score the shortbread into thin wedges. Let cool completely before cutting the wedges.

---

2 cups (10 oz/315 g) all-purpose (plain) flour

⅓ cup (3 oz/90 g) granulated sugar, plus 1 tablespoon for sprinkling

⅓ cup (1½ oz/45 g) confectioners' (icing) sugar

2 teaspoons grated lemon zest

¼ teaspoon salt

1 cup (8 oz/250 g) unsalted butter, cut into pieces, at room temperature

MAKES 12–16 WEDGES OR 32 COOKIES

Honey Madeleines

These classic French cookies are perennial favorites. Enclose small stacks in cellophane bags adorned with ribbons. For a special touch, dip the madeleines in melted bittersweet chocolate.

5 tablespoons (2½ oz/75 g) unsalted butter, at room temperature, plus more for brushing

Scant ⅓ cup (3 oz/90 g) superfine (castor) sugar

2 teaspoons brown sugar

Pinch of salt

1 tablespoon honey

2 large eggs

½ cup (2½ oz/75 g) plus 2 tablespoons all-purpose (plain) flour

Scant 1 teaspoon baking powder

1 teaspoon grated orange zest

Confectioners' (icing) sugar for dusting (optional)

MAKES 1 DOZEN STANDARD OR
2 DOZEN MINIATURE MADELEINES

✧ Preheat oven to 350°F (180°C). Have ready a standard 12-mold madeleine pan or a 24-mold miniature madeleine pan.

✧ In a bowl, using a wooden spoon, beat the 5 tablespoons butter until creamy. Beat in the sugars. Stir in the salt and honey. Add the eggs one at a time, beating well after each addition. In another bowl, sift together the flour and baking powder. Add the flour mixture and orange zest to the butter mixture and stir until blended.

✧ Brush the madeleine pan with melted butter and place in the refrigerator for

2 minutes. Brush the molds again with melted butter and lightly dust with flour, tapping out the excess.

✧ Spoon the batter evenly into the prepared molds; do not overfill. Bake the cookies until golden, 6–7 minutes for miniature madeleines, 8–9 minutes for standard madeleines. Let the cookies rest in the pan for a few seconds. Invert the pan onto a work surface and tap the pan to release. Transfer to wire racks to cool. If desired, dust with confectioners' sugar.

Vanilla–Cardamom Wafers

These elegant butter cookies are shaped with a cookie press, a small tool available at cookware stores. The press comes with plates or disks that create various designs, including the ridged ribbons here.

1 cup (8 oz/250 g) unsalted butter, at room temperature

1 cup (8 oz/250 g) sugar

1 large egg

2½ teaspoons vanilla extract (essence)

½ teaspoon ground cardamom

½ teaspoon salt

2½ cups (10 oz/315 g) sifted all-purpose (plain) flour

Confectioners' (icing) sugar for dusting

MAKES ABOUT 3 DOZEN COOKIES

✧ Preheat oven to 375°F (190°C). Have ready 2 ungreased baking sheets.

✧ In a large bowl, using an electric mixer on high speed, beat the butter and sugar until light and fluffy. Beat in the egg, vanilla, cardamom, and salt until blended. Using a wooden spoon, stir in the flour until well blended.

✧ Fill a cookie press with the dough following the manufacturer's instructions. Fit with the ribbon design plate. Press out the dough directly onto the baking sheets in strips 4 inches (10 cm) long. Bake the cookies until golden brown, about 10 minutes.

✧ When the cookies are done, transfer them to wire racks. Sprinkle with confectioners' sugar and let cool.

Vanilla Stars with Chocolate Filling

This recipe yields a constellation of stars, including some that are bite-sized. For added flavor, brush the small stars with beaten egg white and sprinkle with cinnamon sugar before baking.

✧ Preheat oven to 350°F (180°C). Line 3 baking sheets with parchment (baking) paper.

✧ In a bowl, stir the flour, baking powder, and salt until well blended. In a large bowl, using an electric mixer on medium speed, beat the butter and sugar until light and fluffy. Add the egg and vanilla and beat until blended. Reduce the mixer speed to low and gradually beat in the flour mixture just until blended and the dough comes together.

✧ Turn out the dough onto a work surface. Divide in half, gather up each portion, and press into a disk. Wrap 1 disk in plastic wrap and set aside. (If the dough is very soft, wrap both disks and refrigerate until firm, about 30 minutes.)

✧ Place the unwrapped dough disk on a floured work surface and sprinkle with flour. Roll out the dough ¼ inch (6 mm) thick, sprinkling more flour under and over the dough as needed to prevent sticking.

✧ Using a 2¾-inch (7-cm) star-shaped cookie cutter, cut out as many stars as possible, cutting them close together. Pull the scraps of dough from the shapes and set aside. Using an offset spatula, carefully transfer the cookies to a prepared baking sheet, spacing them about 1 inch (2.5 cm) apart. Gather up the reserved dough scraps and gently press them into a disk. Repeat the rolling and cutting with the scraps and the second dough disk, cutting out 2¾-inch stars. Using a 1½-inch (4-cm) star-shaped cookie cutter, cut out the centers of the larger stars. Transfer the star-shaped centers to another prepared baking sheet and the cutout cookies to the remaining sheet.

✧ Bake the cookies until lightly browned at the edges, about 8 minutes for the small stars, about 9 minutes for the cutout stars, and about 10 minutes for the large stars. Let the cookies cool on the baking sheets on wire racks for 15 minutes. Transfer to the racks to cool completely.

✧ Combine the chocolate and cream in a small heatproof bowl. Set over (not touching) simmering water and stir until the chocolate is melted and smooth. Remove from the heat. Spread about ½ teaspoon of the chocolate mixture on the underside of each large solid star and top with a cutout star, placing the underside down. Press gently. Place the sandwich cookies on a wire rack until the filling is set, about 20 minutes.

¾ cup (4 oz/125 g) all-purpose
(plain) flour

½ teaspoon baking powder

¼ teaspoon salt

½ cup (4 oz/125 g) unsalted butter,
at room temperature

1 cup (8 oz/250 g) sugar

1 large egg

1½ teaspoons vanilla
extract (essence)

2 oz (60 g) bittersweet or semisweet
(plain) chocolate, chopped

2 tablespoons heavy (double) cream

MAKES ABOUT 2 DOZEN SANDWICH
COOKIES AND 2 DOZEN SMALL STARS

Tiny Chocolate and Toffee Cookies

A contemporary twist on a classic chocolate chip cookie, this version is filled with chunks of both semisweet chocolate and toffee. Anyone on your gift list would cherish a tin of these dainty cookies.

¾ cup (6 oz/185 g) firmly packed brown sugar

½ cup (4 oz/125 g) unsalted butter, at room temperature

1 teaspoon vanilla extract (essence)

1 large egg

1¼ cups (6½ oz/200 g) all-purpose (plain) flour

½ teaspoon baking soda (bicarbonate of soda)

¼ teaspoon salt

6 oz (185 g) semisweet (plain) chocolate, cut into ⅓-inch (9-mm) pieces

1 cup (5 oz/155 g) chopped chocolate-covered toffee

MAKES ABOUT 3½ DOZEN COOKIES

✧ Preheat oven to 375°F (190°C). Have ready 2 ungreased baking sheets.

✧ In a large bowl, using an electric mixer on high speed, beat the brown sugar, butter, and vanilla until light and fluffy. Beat in the egg. In another bowl, sift together the flour, baking soda, and salt. Add the flour mixture to the butter mixture and mix on low speed just until blended. Mix in the chocolate and toffee. Drop the dough by heaping teaspoonfuls onto the baking sheets, spacing the cookies about 2 inches (5 cm) apart.

✧ Bake the cookies until golden brown, about 10 minutes, switching the pans and rotating them a half turn halfway through baking. Transfer the cookies to wire racks to cool completely.

Chewy Ginger-Molasses Cookies

Firm, yet chewy, these cookies will keep well for up to 2 weeks, making them a practical and tasty gift from your kitchen. For an even richer color and more intense flavor, use dark molasses.

✧ Preheat oven to 375°F (190°C). Lightly grease 2 baking sheets.

✧ In a large bowl, combine the flour, baking soda, cinnamon, cloves, salt, and ginger and whisk to mix well. Set aside.

✧ In another large bowl, using an electric mixer on high speed, beat the butter and brown sugar until light and fluffy. Beat in the egg and molasses until well blended. Stir in the flour mixture a little at a time until well blended.

✧ Put the granulated sugar in a small, shallow bowl. Shape the dough into walnut-sized balls, and dip the top of each ball in the granulated sugar.

✧ Arrange the balls, sugar side up, on the prepared baking sheets, spacing them about 1 inch (2.5 cm) apart. Bake the cookies until firm to the touch, 10–12 minutes. Transfer to wire racks to cool.

2½ cups (12½ oz/390 g) all-purpose (plain) flour

2 teaspoons baking soda (bicarbonate of soda)

1 teaspoon ground cinnamon

1 teaspoon ground cloves

¼ teaspoon salt

1 tablespoon peeled and grated fresh ginger

¾ cup (6 oz/185 g) unsalted butter, at room temperature

1 cup (7 oz/220 g) firmly packed brown sugar

1 large egg

¼ cup (2¾ oz/80 g) unsulfured light molasses

½ cup (4 oz/125 g) granulated sugar

MAKES ABOUT 4 DOZEN COOKIES

Almond Meringues

These crunchy, festive treats pack well for gifts. Layer them in a flat box or tin and cover with waxed paper. For a classic flavor, you can add a couple drops of vanilla extract after beating in the sugar.

½ cup (2½ oz/75 g) slivered almonds

3 large egg whites,
at room temperature

½ cup (4 oz/125 g) sugar

MAKES ABOUT 2½ DOZEN MERINGUES

✧ Preheat oven to 350°F (180°C). Spread the almonds on a baking sheet and toast, stirring occasionally, until lightly browned and fragrant, about 8 minutes. Transfer to a small plate to cool, and then finely chop.

✧ Reduce oven temperature to 200°F (95°C). Line 2 baking sheets with parchment (baking) paper.

✧ In a large bowl, using an electric mixer on high speed, beat the egg whites until soft peaks form. Gradually add the sugar, beating until stiff peaks form. Using a rubber spatula, fold in the almonds.

✧ Spoon the meringue into a pastry bag fitted with a ½-inch (12-mm) star tip. Pipe the meringue in mounds about 1½ inches (4 cm) in diameter onto the prepared baking sheets, spacing them about 1½ inches apart.

✧ Bake the meringues until crisp and dry, about 2 hours. Remove from the oven and run a sharp knife under the meringues to loosen them from the paper. Let cool on the baking sheets.

Chocolate Crinkle Cookies

Three different forms of chocolate—unsweetened, chips, and cocoa powder—enrich these soft pillows of sweetness. Use good-quality chocolate and, if possible, Dutch-process cocoa powder.

4 oz (125 g) unsweetened chocolate, chopped

¼ cup (2 oz/60 g) unsalted butter

4 large eggs

2 cups (1 lb/500 g) granulated sugar

1 teaspoon vanilla extract (essence)

1½ cups (7½ oz/235 g) all-purpose (plain) flour

½ cup (1½ oz/45 g) unsweetened cocoa powder

2 teaspoons baking powder

¼ teaspoon salt

1½ cups (9 oz/280 g) miniature semisweet (plain) chocolate chips

½ cup (3½ oz/105 g) confectioners' (icing) sugar

MAKES ABOUT 2½ DOZEN COOKIES

✧ Combine the unsweetened chocolate and the butter in the top pan of a double boiler or in a heatproof bowl. Set over (not touching) simmering water and stir until the chocolate and butter are melted and smooth. Remove from the heat and let cool slightly.

✧ In a large bowl, using an electric mixer on medium speed, beat the eggs, granulated sugar, and vanilla until light in color and thick, about 3 minutes. Add the melted chocolate mixture, reduce the mixer speed to low, and beat until blended. In a bowl, stir together the flour, cocoa powder, baking powder, and salt. Add the flour mixture to the chocolate mixture and beat until blended. Mix in the chocolate chips. Cover the bowl and refrigerate until the dough is firm enough to roll into balls, about 2 hours.

✧ Preheat oven to 325°F (165°C). Line 2 baking sheets with parchment (baking) paper. Sift the confectioners' sugar into a bowl.

✧ Roll rounded tablespoonfuls of the dough into 1½-inch (4-cm) balls. Roll each ball in the confectioners' sugar to coat completely. Arrange the balls on the prepared baking sheets, spacing them 3 inches (7.5 cm) apart. Set them firmly on the parchment paper so they stay in place.

✧ Bake the cookies, 1 sheet at a time, until the tops are puffed and crinkled and feel firm when lightly touched, 13–17 minutes. Let the cookies cool on the baking sheet on a wire rack for 5 minutes. Transfer to the rack to cool completely.

Baci

These plump chocolate-sandwich bites ("kisses" in Italian) are the size of truffles. To package them as gifts, arrange them in a box or egg carton on a nest of waxed paper. They will keep for up to 1 week.

1 cup (8 oz/250 g) plus
2 tablespoons unsalted butter,
at room temperature

½ cup (2 oz/60 g) confectioners'
(icing) sugar

½ teaspoon salt

1 tablespoon rum

2 cups (10 oz/315 g) all-purpose
(plain) flour

2 oz (60 g) semisweet
(plain) chocolate

MAKES ABOUT 2 DOZEN COOKIES

✦ In a large bowl, using an electric mixer on medium speed, beat the 1 cup butter, the confectioners' sugar, and the salt until light and fluffy. Beat in the rum. Stir in the flour until smooth and well blended. Cover and refrigerate the dough until firm, about 1 hour.

✦ Preheat oven to 350°F (180°C). Have ready 2 ungreased baking sheets.

✦ Roll teaspoonfuls of the dough into balls and arrange on the baking sheets, spacing them about 1 inch (2.5 cm) apart.

✦ Bake the cookies until firm but not browned, 10–12 minutes. Transfer to wire racks to cool completely.

✦ Combine the chocolate and the remaining 2 tablespoons butter in the top pan of a double boiler or in a heatproof bowl. Set over (not touching) simmering water and heat until the chocolate softens. Remove from the heat and stir until the chocolate is smooth. Let cool slightly.

✦ Using a butter knife, spread a small amount of the chocolate on the bottom of a cookie. Place the bottom of a second cookie on the chocolate and press together. Repeat with the remaining cookies. Let cool on the wire racks until the filling is set.

Almond Florentines

A specialty in Italy, these lacy cookies are studded with citrus zest and drizzled with a combination of chocolates. They make handy gifts, as they keep well for up to 2 weeks.

✧ Preheat oven to 350°F (180°C). Line 2 heavy baking sheets with aluminum foil. Lightly butter the foil.

✧ In a heavy saucepan over medium heat, combine the cream, sugars, and butter. Cook, stirring constantly, just until the sugars dissolve and the butter melts. Add the toasted almonds, flour, and citrus zests. Bring to a boil, stirring constantly. Remove from the heat.

✧ Drop the batter by rounded teaspoonfuls (the batter will be runny) onto the prepared baking sheets, spacing the cookies at least 2 inches (5 cm) apart. Bake the cookies until deep brown, about 8 minutes, switching the pans and rotating them a half turn halfway through baking. Slide the foil off each sheet with the cookies in place. Line the baking sheets again with foil and repeat with the remaining batter.

✧ While all of the cookies are cooling, line the baking sheets again with foil. Carefully peel the cookies off the foil and arrange, smooth side up, on the newly covered baking sheets.

✧ Combine the chocolates in the top pan of a double boiler or in a heatproof bowl. Set over (not touching) simmering water and stir until the chocolates are melted and smooth. Remove from the heat.

✧ Using a butter knife, spread the chocolate over the smooth side of each cookie and return to the baking sheets, chocolate side up. Refrigerate, uncovered, until the chocolate sets.

½ cup (4 fl oz/125 ml) plus 2 tablespoons heavy (double) cream

½ cup (4 oz/125 g) granulated sugar

¼ cup (2 oz/60 g) firmly packed brown sugar

2 tablespoons unsalted butter

1 cup (4 oz/125 g) sliced (flaked) almonds, toasted

¼ cup (1½ oz/45 g) all-purpose (plain) flour

1 tablespoon grated orange zest

2 teaspoons grated lemon zest

4½ oz (140 g) semisweet (plain) chocolate, chopped

½ oz (15 g) unsweetened chocolate, chopped

MAKES ABOUT 3 DOZEN COOKIES

Chocolate-Peppermint Cookies

Snowy white confectioners' sugar covers these dark chocolate cookies. For a special holiday treatment, they are given a final coating of crushed peppermint candies.

4 oz (125 g) unsweetened chocolate, coarsely chopped

2 cups (10 oz/315 g) all-purpose (plain) flour

2 teaspoons baking powder

¼ teaspoon salt

3 large eggs

1½ cups (12 oz/375 g) granulated sugar

½ cup (4 fl oz/125 ml) canola, sunflower, or other light vegetable oil

2 teaspoons vanilla extract (essence)

20–24 red-and-white peppermint candies

1 cup (4 oz/125 g) confectioners' (icing) sugar

MAKES ABOUT 4 DOZEN COOKIES

✧ Put the chocolate in the top pan of a double boiler or in a heatproof bowl. Set over (not touching) simmering water and stir until the chocolate is melted and smooth. Remove from the heat and let cool slightly.

✧ In a large bowl, stir together the flour, baking powder, and salt. In another large bowl, using an electric mixer on high speed, beat the eggs and granulated sugar until well blended. Add the oil, vanilla, and melted chocolate and beat until well blended. Stir in the flour mixture just until fully incorporated. Cover and refrigerate until the dough is firm enough to shape, at least 2 hours or up to 24 hours.

✧ Preheat oven to 350°F (180°C). Have ready 2 ungreased baking sheets.

✧ Place the peppermint candies between 2 sheets of aluminum foil and strike them with a rolling pin, breaking them into large pieces. Roll the candies with the rolling pin to crush them into small pieces.

✧ Put the confectioners' sugar in a shallow bowl. Pinch off pieces of dough and roll into balls about 1 inch (2.5 cm) in diameter. Roll each ball in the confectioners' sugar, coating evenly. Arrange the balls on the baking sheets, spacing them 1 inch apart.

✧ Bake the cookies until they have puffed up and their surfaces crack, showing the chocolate inside, 8–10 minutes. Let cool slightly on the pan, and then gently press some of the crushed peppermint all over each cookie. Transfer to wire racks to cool completely.

CAKES, BARS
& BREADS

Triple-Ginger Gingerbread

When dusting the gingerbreads with sugar, you can use a doily or other stencil to create a pretty design. Baked in round pans, the gingerbreads are cut into wedges, great shapes for packaging as gifts.

✧ Preheat oven to 350°F (180°C). Grease two 8-by-2-inch (20-by-5-cm) round cake pans. In a bowl, whisk together the apple juice, molasses, vinegar, crystallized ginger, and fresh ginger. In a large bowl, sift together the flour, brown sugar, ground ginger, baking soda, and salt. Make a well in the center of the flour mixture. Pour in the oil and the molasses mixture and combine with a rubber spatula just until blended.

✧ Divide the batter evenly between the prepared pans and smooth the tops. Bake until a toothpick inserted in the center comes out clean, about 30 minutes. Let cool completely in the pans on wire racks. Turn out the gingerbreads onto the racks and sift confectioners' sugar over the top.

1 cup (8 fl oz/250 ml) apple juice or water, heated

½ cup (5½ oz/170 g) dark molasses

2 tablespoons cider vinegar

2 tablespoons chopped crystallized ginger

1 tablespoon peeled and grated fresh ginger

3 cups (15 oz/470 g) all-purpose (plain) flour

1 cup (7 oz/220 g) firmly packed brown sugar

2 teaspoons ground ginger

2 teaspoons baking soda (bicarbonate of soda)

½ teaspoon salt

⅔ cup (5 fl oz/160 ml) sunflower oil

Confectioners' (icing) sugar for dusting

MAKES 2 GINGERBREADS

Kugelhopf

Traditionally baked in a tall ring mold of the same name, this fruit-and-nut-studded yeast cake is thought to have originated in Austria, although cooks in France and elsewhere claim it as well.

½ cup (4 fl oz/125 ml) warm water (105°–115°F/40°–46°C)

¾ cup (6 oz/185 g) plus 1 teaspoon granulated sugar

5 teaspoons (2 packages) active dry yeast

1 cup (8 oz/250 g) unsalted butter, at room temperature

6 large eggs

1 tablespoon grated lemon zest

1 teaspoon salt

1 teaspoon vanilla extract (essence)

4 cups (1¼ lb/625 g) all-purpose (plain) flour, sifted

1 cup (6 oz/185 g) golden raisins (sultanas)

½ cup (2½ oz/75 g) slivered almonds, toasted

Confectioners' (icing) sugar for dusting

MAKES 1 KUGELHOPF

✧ In a small bowl, stir together the warm water and the 1 teaspoon granulated sugar. Sprinkle with the yeast and let stand until foamy, about 5 minutes. In a large bowl, using an electric mixer on high speed, beat the butter and the ¾ cup granulated sugar until light and fluffy. Beat in the eggs, one at a time. Beat in the lemon zest, salt, and vanilla. Add the yeast mixture and gradually beat in 2 cups (10 oz/315 g) of the flour. Reduce the mixer speed to medium and beat for 5 minutes. Gradually add the remaining flour and beat until the dough is elastic. Stir in the raisins and almonds.

✧ Transfer the dough to a buttered large bowl, cover with a kitchen towel, and let rise in a warm place until doubled in bulk, 1½–2 hours. Grease and flour a 2½-qt (2.5-l) kugelhopf or Bundt pan.

✧ Punch down the dough, then transfer to the prepared pan and cover with a towel. Let rise in a warm place until the dough comes to within ½ inch (12 mm) of the rim, about 1 hour.

✧ Preheat oven to 475°F (245°C). Bake for 10 minutes. Reduce oven temperature to 350°F (180°C) and bake until a toothpick inserted in the center comes out clean, 30–35 minutes. Let cool in the pan on a wire rack for 5 minutes. Turn out the kugelhopf onto the rack to cool completely. Sift confectioners' sugar over the top.

Packaging Ideas

CELLOPHANE WRAP • CONTAINERS • RIBBON

Baked goods can be dressed up for the holidays with festive and creative packaging. Choose wrapping that matches the tastes of the recipient.

Tea cakes A tea cup or mug makes a perfect package for a stack of shortbread. Attach a spoon, or even a bundle of tea, with a fancy ribbon.

Bread board Use a shallow wooden tray or board for giving mini loaves of bread. Wrap in cellophane and tie on a sprig of rosemary or another herb.

Dressed-up box Colorful boxes of assorted sizes can hold cookies and other baked goods. Line with tissue cut in an attractive pattern.

Currant, Lemon, and Ginger Cake

The cake is made a day ahead so that the lively flavors have time to develop. Once the cake is tightly wrapped, it can be stored at room temperature for up to 3 days.

✧ Position a rack in the lower third of oven and preheat oven to 350°F (180°C). Grease and flour a 7-cup (56–fl oz/1.75-l) tube pan or Bundt pan.

✧ In a bowl, sift together the flour, cinnamon, ground ginger, and baking soda. Stir in the currants and crystallized ginger.

✧ Using an electric mixer set on high speed, beat the butter and granulated sugar in a large bowl until light and fluffy. Add the eggs, one at a time, beating well after each addition. Mix in the lemon zest. Reduce the mixer speed to low, add the flour mixture and lemon juice, and mix just until blended. Pour the batter into the prepared pan and smooth the top.

✧ Bake until a toothpick inserted near the center comes out clean, about 50 minutes. Let the cake cool in the pan on a wire rack for 20 minutes. Turn out the cake onto the rack and let cool completely. Wrap tightly with aluminum foil and let stand overnight at room temperature.

✧ Sift confectioners' sugar over the top.

1½ cups (7½ oz/235 g) all-purpose (plain) flour

1 teaspoon ground cinnamon

1 teaspoon ground ginger

½ teaspoon baking soda (bicarbonate of soda)

1½ cups (9 oz/280 g) dried currants

½ cup (1 oz/30 g) chopped crystallized ginger

¾ cup (6 oz/185 g) plus 2 tablespoons unsalted butter, at room temperature

¾ cup (6 oz/185 g) granulated sugar

3 eggs

2½ teaspoons finely grated lemon zest

¼ cup (2 fl oz/60 ml) fresh lemon juice

Confectioners' (icing) sugar for dusting

MAKES 1 CAKE

Fig and Walnut Quick Bread

Chewy and sweet, figs add extra moisture and texture to this bread. You can substitute coarsely chopped pitted dates or use a combination of dates and figs. The bread keeps for up to 4 days.

2 cups (10 oz/315 g) all-purpose (plain) flour

2 teaspoons baking powder

¼ teaspoon salt

6 tablespoons (3 oz/90 g) unsalted butter, at room temperature

⅔ cup (5 oz/155 g) firmly packed brown sugar

2 large eggs

2 teaspoons grated lemon zest

2 cups (16 fl oz/500 ml) whole milk

½ lb (250 g) dried figs, coarsely chopped

⅔ cup (2½ oz/75 g) chopped walnuts

MAKES 1 LOAF

◇ Preheat oven to 350°F (180°C). Grease an 8½-by-4½-inch (21.5-by-11.5-cm) loaf pan.

◇ In a large bowl, stir together the flour, baking powder, and salt.

◇ In another large bowl, using an electric mixer on high speed, beat the butter and brown sugar until fluffy. Beat in the eggs until well blended. Stir in the lemon zest. Stir the flour mixture into the butter mixture in three additions alternately with the milk in two additions, beginning and ending with the flour mixture and mixing until well blended. Stir in the figs and walnuts. Spoon the batter into the prepared pan and smooth the top.

◇ Bake until the bread is golden and puffed and a toothpick inserted in the center comes out clean, about 50 minutes. Let cool in the pan on a wire rack for 15 minutes. Turn out the bread onto the rack and let cool completely.

Pistachio and Dried-Cherry Biscotti

With their green pistachios and red cherries, these crisp biscotti are already decorated for the holidays. They keep well in an airtight container for 1 week, making them a good choice to bake ahead.

2 cups (10 oz/315 g) all-purpose (plain) flour

1 teaspoon baking powder

¼ teaspoon salt

1 cup (8 oz/250 g) sugar

2 teaspoons grated orange zest

½ cup (4 oz/125 g) unsalted butter, at room temperature

2 large eggs

1 teaspoon vanilla extract (essence)

¾ cup (3 oz/90 g) unsalted pistachio nuts, toasted and coarsely chopped

½ cup (3 oz/90 g) dried tart cherries, coarsely chopped

MAKES 4 DOZEN BISCOTTI

✧ Preheat oven to 350°F (180°C). Line a baking sheet with parchment (baking) paper. Have ready another, unlined baking sheet.

✧ In a bowl, stir together the flour, baking powder, and salt. In a food processor, combine the sugar and orange zest and process until finely chopped. Transfer to a large bowl and add the butter. Using an electric mixer on medium speed, beat until light and fluffy. Add the eggs, one at a time, beating well after each addition. Beat in the vanilla. Reduce the mixer speed to low and gradually beat in the flour mixture just until blended. Using a rubber spatula, fold in the pistachios and dried cherries.

✧ Divide the dough in half and place both portions on the parchment-lined baking sheet. Quickly form each half into a log 12 inches (30 cm) long and 2 inches (5 cm) in diameter. Arrange the logs at least 3 inches (7.5 cm) apart on the baking sheet and smooth them with dampened fingers. Bake the logs, rotating the pan a half turn halfway through the baking time, until the logs begin to crack on top, about 35 minutes. Let cool on the baking sheet for 10 minutes. Leave the oven on.

✧ Transfer the logs to a cutting board and discard the parchment. Using a sharp serrated knife, cut each log on the diagonal into slices ½ inch (12 mm) thick. Arrange the slices flat on the 2 unlined baking sheets. Bake until lightly browned on both sides, about 16 minutes. Let the biscotti cool on the baking sheets on a wire rack.

Mini Chocolate-Mint Cupcakes

Resembling brownies, these miniature cupcakes have a moist, fudgy texture. As a bonus, both the batter and the frosting are flavored with peppermint. The frosting can be spread or piped on the cupcakes.

✦ Preheat oven to 350°F (180°C). Line a 24-cup mini muffin pan with liners.

✦ Combine the chocolate and butter in the top pan of a double boiler or in a heatproof bowl. Set over (not touching) simmering water, and stir until the chocolate and butter are melted and smooth. Remove from the heat, scrape into a bowl, and let cool to room temperature.

✦ Stir the sugar into the chocolate mixture. Whisk in the eggs, one at a time, until combined. Whisk in the vanilla and peppermint extracts and then the salt. Using a rubber spatula, fold in the flour; do not overmix. Spoon the batter into the prepared muffin cups, filling each about three-fourths full. Bake until a toothpick inserted in the center of a cupcake comes out with only a few moist crumbs attached, 18–20 minutes. Let the cupcakes cool completely in the pan on a wire rack, about 45 minutes.

✦ Meanwhile, make the buttercream: Melt the chocolate, following the process above.

Remove from the heat and let cool. In a large, clean heatproof bowl, combine the egg whites and sugar. Set the bowl over (not touching) simmering water and heat the mixture, whisking constantly, until the sugar has completely dissolved and the mixture is very warm to the touch, about 2 minutes. Remove the bowl from the heat. Using an electric mixer on high speed, beat the egg white mixture until it is fluffy, cooled to room temperature, and holds stiff peaks but does not look dry, about 6 minutes.

✦ With the mixer on medium-low speed, add the salt and the butter, a few pieces at a time, beating well after each addition. If the frosting appears to separate after all the butter is added, beat on high speed until it is smooth and creamy, 3–5 minutes longer. Add the melted chocolate, cocoa powder, and peppermint extract and beat until well combined.

✦ Using a table knife or pastry bag, spread or pipe the frosting on the cupcakes.

4 oz (125 g) bittersweet chocolate, chopped

4 tablespoons (2 oz/60 g) unsalted butter, cut into 4 pieces

¾ cup (6 oz/185 g) sugar

2 large eggs, at room temperature

½ teaspoon vanilla extract (essence)

¼ teaspoon peppermint extract (essence)

¼ teaspoon salt

¼ cup (1½ oz/45 g) plus 2 tablespoons all-purpose (plain) flour

Chocolate-Mint Buttercream

4 oz (125 g) semisweet (plain) chocolate

3 large egg whites, at room temperature

¾ cup (6 oz/185 g) sugar

Pinch of salt

1 cup (8 oz/250 g) unsalted butter, cut into 16 pieces, at room temperature

2 tablespoons unsweetened cocoa powder, preferably Dutch process

½ teaspoon peppermint extract (essence)

MAKES 24 CUPCAKES

Chocolate Shortbread

Shortbread, a specialty of Scotland, tastes best when it is both noticeably rich and delicately crumbly. Give this especially rich chocolate version with a tin of the recipient's favorite tea.

4 cups (1¼ lb/625 g) all-purpose (plain) flour

⅓ cup (1 oz/30 g) unsweetened cocoa powder, preferably Dutch process

1 cup (8 oz/250 g) unsalted butter, at room temperature

1¼ cups (5 oz/155 g) confectioners' (icing) sugar

¼ teaspoon salt

1 teaspoon vanilla extract (essence)

MAKES 3 DOZEN BARS

✧ Preheat oven to 325°F (165°C). Lightly grease a straight-sided 9-inch (23-cm) square baking pan and line the bottom and sides with parchment (baking) paper.

✧ In a bowl, sift together the flour and cocoa powder. In a large bowl, using an electric mixer on medium speed, beat the butter, confectioners' sugar, and salt until light and fluffy. Add the vanilla and beat until blended. Reduce the mixer speed to low and gradually beat in the flour mixture just until blended.

✧ Scrape the dough into the prepared baking pan. Using lightly floured fingertips, pat the dough into an even layer. Using a ruler and a knife, score the dough into 1-by-2¼-inch (2.5-by-5.5-cm) bars. Positioning the tines of a fork on an angle, prick each bar twice all the way through the dough. Bake until the top appears dry, 35–40 minutes.

✧ Transfer the pan to a wire rack and let the shortbread stand until cool enough to handle yet still warm, 5–7 minutes. Using the score marks as a guide, cut the bars through to the pan bottom and let cool in the pan. Lifting the parchment, remove the bars from the pan.

Espresso Triple-Chocolate Brownies

These luscious brownies feature three kinds of chocolate and a hint of espresso. You can substitute walnuts or pecans for the macadamia nuts, or omit them altogether.

✧ Preheat oven to 375°F (190°C). Line an 8-inch (20-cm) square baking pan with 2-inch (5-cm) sides with aluminum foil, letting the foil overhang the sides. Grease the foil.

✧ In a large, heavy saucepan over low heat, combine the butter, unsweetened chocolate, and espresso powder. Stir until the butter and chocolate are melted and smooth. Remove from the heat and stir in the brown sugar until smooth. Using a wooden spoon, beat in the eggs one at a time, beating well after each addition. Beat in the flour and salt until blended. Using a rubber spatula, fold in the nuts and the bittersweet and white chocolates just until evenly distributed. Using the rubber spatula, scrape the batter into the prepared pan and smooth the top.

✧ Bake until the brownies pull away from the sides of the pan, about 40 minutes. Let cool completely in the pan on a wire rack. Cut into bars and, using the foil, lift them from the pan.

½ cup (4 oz/125 g) unsalted butter, cut into pieces

4 oz (125 g) unsweetened chocolate, coarsely chopped

3 tablespoons instant espresso powder or ground beans

2 cups (14 oz/440 g) firmly packed brown sugar

4 large eggs

1 cup (5 oz/155 g) all-purpose (plain) flour

¼ teaspoon salt

½ cup (2½ oz/75 g) macadamia nuts, chopped

3 oz (90 g) bittersweet chocolate, chopped

3 oz (90 g) white chocolate, chopped

MAKES ABOUT 16 BARS

White Chocolate Blondies

A rich take on a classic favorite, these blondies have a caramel glaze and are studded with macadamia nuts. You can top them with chocolate glaze or use a different nut if desired.

½ cup (4 oz/125 g) unsalted butter, at room temperature

1¼ cups (9 oz/280 g) firmly packed brown sugar

2 teaspoons instant espresso powder

1 teaspoon vanilla extract (essence)

2 large eggs

1 cup (5 oz/155 g) all-purpose (plain) flour

¾ cup (3½ oz/105 g) macadamia nuts, coarsely chopped

3–4 oz (90–125 g) white chocolate, coarsely chopped

½ lb (250 g) caramel candies (about 1 cup packed)

MAKES ABOUT 16 BARS

✧ Preheat oven to 350°F (180°C). Grease an 8-inch (20-cm) square baking pan.

✧ In a large bowl, using an electric mixer on high speed, beat the butter, brown sugar, espresso powder, and vanilla until light and fluffy. Beat in the eggs one at a time until incorporated, then continue beating at high speed until very fluffy, about 2 minutes. Reduce the mixer speed to low, add the flour, and mix in until well blended. Using a rubber spatula, fold in the nuts and chocolate and mix just until blended. Using the rubber spatula, scrape the batter into the prepared pan and smooth the top.

✧ Bake until a toothpick inserted in the center comes out clean, about 40 minutes. Let cool in the pan on a wire rack.

✧ In a small, heavy saucepan over low heat, combine the caramels and ¼ cup (2 fl oz/ 60 ml) water. Stir constantly until the caramels melt and the mixture is smooth. Remove from the heat.

✧ Using a fork or spoon, slowly drizzle the hot caramel glaze over the blondies. Or, spread the glaze using a table knife. Let the blondies stand until cool, about 30 minutes. Cut into bars.

Raspberry and Hazelnut Linzer Bars

These layered treats call for many of the same ingredients used in the famed Linzertorte, thus their name. They can be cut into squares or into small triangles, and are delicious served with coffee or tea.

✧ Preheat oven to 350°F (180°C). Lightly grease a 9-by-13-inch (23-by-33-cm) baking pan. Line the bottom and sides with parchment (baking) paper, then lightly grease and flour the paper.

✧ In a bowl, stir together the flour, hazelnuts, cinnamon, cloves, and salt. In a large bowl, using an electric mixer on medium speed, beat the butter, sugar, and lemon zest until light and fluffy. Add the eggs one at a time and beat just until blended. Reduce the mixer speed to low and add the flour mixture in 2 batches, beating well after each addition.

✧ Scoop two-thirds of the dough into the prepared pan. Using lightly floured fingertips, pat the dough into an even layer. Spread the preserves evenly over the dough. Dollop the remaining dough in spoonfuls over the preserves. Press the dough with floured fingers to flatten slightly. The top dough layer should not cover the preserves completely.

✧ Bake until the top is browned and the preserves are bubbling, about 50 minutes. Transfer to a wire rack to cool completely. Using the parchment, lift out the whole cookie and transfer to a cutting board. Trim away the edges (about ½ inch/12 mm on all sides) and cut into 2-inch (5-cm) squares. If desired, cut each square into 2 triangles.

1⅔ cups (8½ oz/265 g) all-purpose (plain) flour

1⅓ cups (5 oz/155 g) ground toasted hazelnuts (filberts)

1 teaspoon ground cinnamon

½ teaspoon ground cloves

¼ teaspoon salt

1 cup (8 oz/250 g) unsalted butter, at room temperature

1½ cups (12 oz/375 g) sugar

½ teaspoon grated lemon zest

2 large eggs

1 cup (10 oz/315 g) seedless raspberry preserves

MAKES 2 DOZEN SQUARES OR
4 DOZEN TRIANGLES

Key Lime Bars

These sweet–tart treats are a refreshing version of classic lemon bars. If you cannot find Key limes, substitute Persian limes. You can also use Meyer lemons for a slightly different citrus flavor.

2½ cups (12½ oz/390 g) all-purpose (plain) flour, plus ¼ cup (1½ oz/45 g)

½ cup (2 oz/60 g) confectioners' (icing) sugar, plus extra for dusting

½ cup (4 oz/125 g) chilled unsalted butter, cut into ½-inch (12-mm) cubes

3 oz (90 g) chilled cream cheese, cut into ½-inch (12-mm) cubes

¼ teaspoon almond extract (essence)

4 large eggs

2 cups (1 lb/500 g) granulated sugar

½ cup (4 fl oz/125 ml) fresh Key lime juice (8–10 limes)

Grated zest of 4 Key limes (about 1 tablespoon)

1 teaspoon vanilla extract (essence)

MAKES 3 DOZEN BARS

✧ Preheat oven to 350°F (180°C). Have ready a 9-by-13-by-2-inch (23-by-33-by-5-cm) baking pan.

✧ In a food processor, combine the 2½ cups flour, ½ cup confectioners' sugar, butter, cream cheese, and almond extract. Pulse just until the mixture is crumbly but holds together when squeezed between your fingers. Working quickly, transfer the dough to the pan and press evenly into the bottom and ½ inch (12 mm) up the sides. Bake until lightly browned, 20–25 minutes. Transfer to a wire rack and let cool for 10 minutes. Leave the oven on.

✧ In a large bowl, whisk together the eggs, granulated sugar, lime juice and zest, vanilla, and the ¼ cup flour. Pour over the warm baked crust.

✧ Bake until the center is set and no longer sticky, 22–24 minutes. The filling will be slightly soft when touched, similar to a pie filling. Transfer to a wire rack to cool completely. Cover and refrigerate for at least 6 hours or up to overnight.

✧ Cut evenly into bars. Sift confectioners' sugar over the tops. Store in the refrigerator.

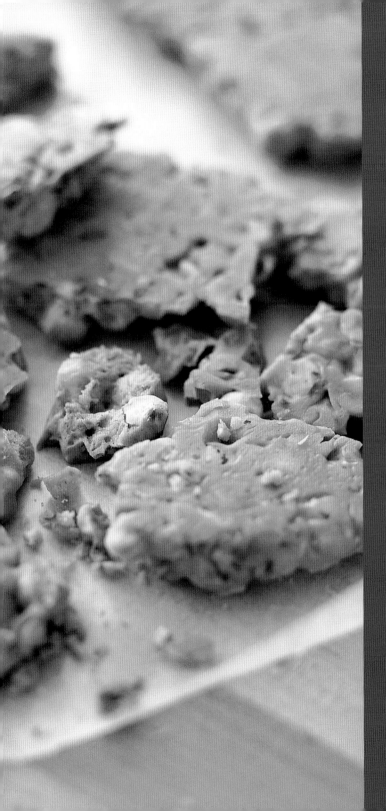

CANDIES & CONFECTIONS

Chocolate-Marshmallow Fudge

This creamy, rich fudge is lightened by marshmallows. The uncut fudge will keep in the refrigerator for 1 week, tightly wrapped in foil. Cut into bars before packing into gift boxes.

✧ Lightly grease an 8-inch (20-cm) square baking pan.

✧ In a large, heavy saucepan over medium heat, combine the butter, sugars, corn syrup, half-and-half, and salt and bring to a boil, stirring constantly. Using a pastry brush dipped in hot water, brush down any sugar crystals that form on the sides of the pan. Boil for 2½ minutes, add the chocolate, and stir until melted and well blended. Clip a candy thermometer to the side of the pan and continue to boil, without stirring, until the thermometer reads 234°F (112°C), 7–10 minutes. Remove from the heat and let cool until almost room temperature, or 110°F (43°C) on the thermometer, about 30 minutes.

✧ Using an electric mixer, beat the fudge until the color dulls and the fudge is creamy, 2–3 minutes. Stir in the walnuts.

✧ Sprinkle the marshmallows in the prepared pan and spoon the fudge over them. Lay a piece of plastic wrap over the fudge and, using your hands, press the fudge down firmly into the marshmallows. Remove the plastic and smooth the surface of the fudge with a spatula. Cover the pan with aluminum foil and refrigerate until firm, about 6 hours. Cut into 2-inch (5-cm) bars, or any shape desired.

---

4 tablespoons (2 oz/60 g) unsalted butter, melted

1 cup (7 oz/220 g) firmly packed brown sugar

1 cup (8 oz/250 g) granulated sugar

¼ cup (2½ oz/75 g) light corn syrup

½ cup (4 fl oz/125 ml) half-and-half (half cream)

⅛ teaspoon salt

4 oz (125 g) bittersweet or semisweet (plain) chocolate, coarsely chopped

½ cup (2 oz/60 g) chopped walnuts, toasted

1½ cups (2½ oz/75 g) miniature marshmallows

MAKES 32 BARS

Chocolate Truffles

A high-quality chocolate (look for a high percentage of cacao) is the best choice for making these truffles. They can be dusted with cocoa powder, or coated with melted chocolate and sprinkled with sea salt.

2 cups (16 fl oz/500 ml) heavy (double) cream

1 lb (500 g) bittersweet or semisweet (plain) chocolate, finely chopped

½ cup (4 oz/125 g) unsalted butter, at room temperature

½ cup (4 fl oz/125 ml) Cognac, Grand Marnier, or other liqueur

Unsweetened cocoa powder, preferably Dutch process, for sprinkling (optional)

8 oz (250 g) semisweet (plain) chocolate, coarsely chopped (optional)

Sea salt, for sprinkling (optional)

MAKES ABOUT 3 DOZEN TRUFFLES

✧ In a saucepan over medium heat, bring the cream to a boil. Remove from the heat, add the chopped chocolate, and stir until it is melted, smooth, and shiny. Beat in the butter until smooth. Pour into a bowl and stir in the liqueur. Refrigerate until set, about 1 hour.

✧ Line a baking sheet with parchment (baking) paper. Using a spoon, scoop out 1-inch (2.5-cm) balls of the chocolate and place on the prepared baking sheet. Refrigerate until chilled, about 30 minutes.

✧ To shape the truffles, roll each ball between your palms until it is perfectly round. Sprinkle generously with cocoa powder, if using.

✧ If using a chocolate coating, put the chocolate in the top pan of a double boiler or in a heatproof bowl. Set over (not touching) simmering water and stir until the chocolate is melted and smooth. Remove from the heat. Line 2 baking sheets with waxed paper and top each with a wire rack. Using a fork, dip the truffles one at a time into the chocolate, turning to coat. Transfer to the wire racks to cool. Add a sprinkle of sea salt to the top of each truffle, if using, and let stand until the chocolate is set.

✧ Store in layers, separated by waxed paper, in an airtight container in the refrigerator for up to 1 week.

Holiday Candy Cones

CONES • CANDIES • CELLOPHANE WRAP • RIBBON

I Gather all of your supplies: a mix of holiday candy (such as truffles, bonbons, peppermints, and chocolates), decorative cones, a roll of cellophane, and a selection of seasonal ribbon.

2 Cut squares of cellophane about twice the size of the cones. Carefully wrap each cone, using tape or glue to adhere the edges of the cellophane to the cone. Leave plenty of cellophane at the top to cover the sweets.

3 Fill each cone with sweets, mixing varieties if desired. Gather the cellophane just above the sweets, twist gently, and tie with ribbon. Trim the top of the cellophane attractively, if desired.

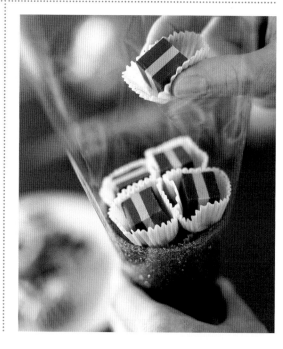

Candied Grapefruit Peel

This old-fashioned sweet was once a holiday gift from one family to another. For a fancy touch, dip one end of each peel into melted chocolate and let the peels stand on wire racks until the chocolate sets.

2 large ruby red or other grapefruits or 4 oranges

1½ cups (12 oz/375 g) sugar

MAKES ABOUT 3 DOZEN PIECES

✧ Using a sharp knife, cut a thin slice from the top and bottom of each grapefruit to reveal the flesh. Working from the top to the bottom, score through the outer peel and thick white pith to the flesh, spacing the cuts about 1 inch (2.5 cm) apart. Peel the grapefruits. Cut each peel section lengthwise into long strips about ¼ inch (6 mm) wide. (Reserve the flesh for another use.)

✧ In a large saucepan, combine the peels with water to cover by 2 inches (5 cm). Bring to a boil over high heat, then reduce the heat to medium. Simmer, uncovered, until only about 1 inch (2.5 cm) of water remains, about 1 hour. The peels will begin to soften and become translucent. Drain.

✧ When the peels are almost ready, in another saucepan, combine 2 cups (16 fl oz/ 500 ml) water and 1 cup (8 oz/250 g) of the sugar. Bring to a boil over high heat and stir to dissolve the sugar, 3–4 minutes. Remove from the heat and stir in the drained peels. Let stand for 6–8 hours at room temperature.

✧ Return the pan to low heat, bring to a simmer, and cook until the peels have absorbed most of the liquid, about 30 minutes. During the last stages of cooking, watch carefully to prevent scorching.

✧ Using a slotted spoon, transfer the peels to a sheet of waxed paper, spreading them in a single layer. Let stand for about 12 hours to dry slightly.

✧ Place the remaining ½ cup (4 oz/125 g) sugar in a small, shallow bowl. Roll each peel in the sugar to coat. Arrange in a single layer on a fresh piece of waxed paper and let dry for a few hours longer.

✧ Store in layers, separated by waxed paper, in an airtight container at room temperature for up to 2 months.

Pecan–Molasses Toffee

The molasses gives this candy a deep flavor, the nuts lend crunch, and the rich chocolate coating provides an elegant finish. Walnuts, almonds, or hazelnuts (filberts) can be substituted for the pecans.

✧ Grease a small baking sheet. In a heavy 2½-qt (2.5-l) saucepan over low heat, melt the butter. Add the sugars, molasses, and ¼ cup (2 fl oz/60 ml) water and stir until the sugars dissolve. Raise the heat to medium and clip a candy thermometer onto the side of the pan. Cook, stirring slowly but constantly, until the thermometer reads 290°F (143°C), about 15 minutes.

✧ Remove from the heat. Stir in the 1 cup pecans and the cinnamon. Immediately pour the mixture into the prepared pan; do not scrape the residue from the pan bottom. Let stand for 1 minute. Sprinkle the chocolate over the toffee. Let stand for 1 minute to soften. Using the back of a metal spoon, spread the chocolate over the toffee until it is melted. Sprinkle with the ½ cup pecans. Refrigerate uncovered until the toffee is firm, about 2 hours.

✧ Break the toffee into 2-inch (5-cm) pieces. Store in an airtight container in the refrigerator for up to 3 weeks.

1¼ cups (10 oz/315 g) unsalted butter

1 cup (8 oz/250 g) granulated sugar

¼ cup (2 oz/60 g) firmly packed brown sugar

1 tablespoon dark molasses

1 cup (4 oz/125 g) very coarsely chopped pecans, plus ½ cup (2 oz/60 g) medium-fine chopped pecans

½ teaspoon ground cinnamon

6 oz (185 g) bittersweet or semisweet (plain) chocolate, finely chopped

MAKES ABOUT 1½ LB (750 G) TOFFEE

Vanilla Bean Caramels

If you like, you can wrap the caramels in cellophane or colored waxed paper sold at kitchenware shops. They will keep for up to 2 weeks in an airtight container.

½ cup (3½ oz/105 g) firmly packed brown sugar

½ cup (4 oz/125 g) granulated sugar

½ cup (5 oz/155 g) light corn syrup

¼ cup (2 fl oz/60 ml) plus 2 tablespoons whole milk

¼ cup (2 fl oz/60 ml) plus 2 tablespoons condensed milk

¼ cup (2 fl oz/60 ml) heavy (double) cream

¼ cup (2 oz/60 g) unsalted butter

1 vanilla bean, split lengthwise

Pinch of salt

MAKES ABOUT 3 DOZEN CARAMELS

✧ Line an 8-inch (20-cm) square baking pan with aluminum foil, covering the bottom and sides, then grease generously.

✧ In a heavy 3-qt (3-l) saucepan over medium heat, combine the sugars, corn syrup, milks, cream, butter, vanilla bean, and salt. Stir until the sugars dissolve and the mixture comes to a boil. Using a pastry brush dipped in water, brush down the sides of the pan to prevent sugar crystals from forming. Clip a candy thermometer onto the side of the pan. Raise the heat to medium-high and cook, stirring slowly but constantly, until the thermometer reads 240°F (115°C), about 10 minutes.

✧ Remove from the heat. Discard the vanilla bean. Immediately pour the caramel into the prepared pan; do not scrape the residue from the pan bottom. Let cool completely, about 2 hours.

✧ Grease a cutting board. Turn out the cooled caramel onto the board and peel off the foil. Grease a large knife and cut the caramel into strips about 1½ inches (4 cm) wide. Cut the strips crosswise into pieces 1 inch (2.5 cm) long, greasing the knife occasionally to prevent sticking. Wrap each caramel in a 4½-by-6-inch (12-by-15-cm) piece of clear cellophane or colored waxed paper, twisting the ends.

Pine Nut Brittle

The secret to making good brittle is low humidity, since the candy becomes sticky in humid weather. Stored in an airtight container, the brittle will keep for up to 1 week.

✧ Grease a baking sheet. In a bowl, combine the pine nuts, orange zest, butter, and salt.

✧ In a heavy 2-qt (2-l) saucepan over low heat, combine the sugar and ⅓ cup (3 fl oz/ 80 ml) water. Stir until the sugar dissolves. Using a pastry brush dipped in water, brush down the sides of the pan to prevent sugar crystals from forming. Raise the heat to high and bring the mixture to a rolling boil.

Continue to boil without stirring, swirling the pan occasionally, until the mixture turns a deep golden color, about 10 minutes.

✧ Add the nut mixture and stir until coated with the syrup. Immediately pour onto the prepared baking sheet. Spread out slightly with a wooden spoon, forming a thin sheet of brittle. Let cool completely, about 30 minutes. Break into pieces.

1 cup (5 oz/155 g) pine nuts

1 tablespoon finely grated orange zest

1½ teaspoons unsalted butter

¼ teaspoon salt

1 cup (8 oz/250 g) sugar

MAKES ABOUT 10 OZ (315 G) BRITTLE

Caramel-Nut Popcorn

With its three varieties of nuts and sweet caramel glaze, this is a very luxurious popcorn. You can prepare it ahead and store in an airtight container at room temperature for up to 1 week.

3 cups (3 l) freshly popped corn (about ½ cup/3 oz/90 g unpopped)

1 cup (5 oz/155 g) unsalted roasted cashews

1 cup (5 oz/155 g) salted roasted macadamia nuts

1 cup (5½ oz/170 g) whole almonds or 1 cup (4 oz/125 g) pecan halves

1 cup (7 oz/220 g) firmly packed brown sugar

½ cup (5 oz/155 g) light corn syrup

½ cup (4 oz/125 g) unsalted butter

1 tablespoon finely grated orange zest

½ teaspoon salt

1 teaspoon vanilla extract (essence)

½ teaspoon baking soda (bicarbonate of soda)

MAKES ABOUT 4 QT (4 L) POPCORN

✧ Preheat oven to 250°F (120°C). Grease a large roasting pan. Combine the popped corn and all of the nuts in the prepared pan, mixing well. Place in the oven as it heats while you prepare the glaze.

✧ In a large, heavy saucepan over medium heat, combine the brown sugar, corn syrup, butter, orange zest, and salt. Bring to a boil, stirring until the sugar dissolves. Boil for 4 minutes without stirring. Remove from the heat and mix in the vanilla and baking soda. Remove the roasting pan from the oven. Gradually pour the glaze over the popped corn mixture, stirring to coat well.

✧ Bake until the nuts and popcorn are dry, stirring occasionally, about 1 hour. Remove from the oven. Using a metal spatula, loosen the nuts and popcorn from the bottom of the pan. Let cool completely in the pan. Break into clumps.

SAVORY TREATS

Cheese Straws

Zesty, savory cheese straws make an easy and elegant holiday gift. To save time, this recipe calls for purchased puff pastry. The straws will keep for up to 2 weeks in an airtight container.

✧ Preheat oven to 400°F (200°C). Line 2 baking sheets with parchment (baking) paper. In a bowl, toss together the cheeses, dry mustard, cayenne, and black pepper.

✧ Place 1 pastry sheet on a lightly floured surface and gently roll out into a 12-by-10-inch (30-by-25-cm) rectangle. Brush with some of the beaten egg and sprinkle with ½ cup (2 oz/60 g) of the cheese mixture. Flip the sheet so the cheese side is down. Brush with beaten egg and sprinkle with another ½ cup of the cheese mixture.

✧ Using a fluted pastry or pizza wheel, cut the sheet into 24 strips each ½ inch (12 mm) wide and 10 inches (25 cm) long. Twist each strip and set the strips at least 1 inch (2.5 cm) apart on a prepared baking sheet, pressing the ends onto the parchment to secure them and prevent them from untwisting. Repeat with the second pastry sheet and remaining cheese mixture.

✧ Bake until the cheese melts and the straws turn crisp and golden, about 15 minutes. Transfer to a wire rack to cool.

1 cup (4 oz/125 g) finely shredded Cheddar cheese

1 cup (4 oz/125 g) grated Parmesan or pecorino cheese

1 tablespoon dry mustard

½ teaspoon cayenne pepper

½ teaspoon freshly ground black pepper

2 sheets frozen puff pastry, thawed in the refrigerator and unfolded

1 egg, lightly beaten

MAKES ABOUT 4 DOZEN STRAWS

Savory Palmiers

Palmiers are French cookies made from sweetened puff pastry and shaped to suggest palm leaves. The distinctive shape has been borrowed to create these crisp, peppery cheese snacks.

1 cup (4 oz/125 g) grated Parmesan cheese

1 cup (4 oz/125 g) grated pecorino cheese

2 teaspoons dry mustard

½–1 teaspoon cayenne pepper

¼ teaspoon freshly ground black pepper

2 sheets frozen puff pastry, thawed in the refrigerator and unfolded

MAKES ABOUT 3 DOZEN PALMIERS

✧ In a bowl, toss together the cheeses, dry mustard, cayenne, and black pepper.

✧ Place 1 pastry sheet on a lightly floured surface and gently roll out into a 10-by-9¼-inch (25-by-23.5-cm) rectangle. Sprinkle with about ¾ cup (3 oz/90 g) of the cheese mixture. Starting from a long side, lightly roll up the pastry, stopping at the midpoint of the sheet. Roll up the other long side, also stopping at the midpoint. Repeat with the second pastry sheet and ¾ cup of the cheese mixture. Wrap each roll tightly in plastic wrap, place on a baking sheet, and refrigerate or freeze until firm.

✧ Preheat oven to 400°F (200°C). Line 2 baking sheets with parchment (baking) paper. Working with 1 pastry roll at a time, and using a thin, sharp knife, cut off and discard a thin slice from each end to form an even edge. Cut into slices about ½ inch (12 mm) thick. If the dough begins to feel too soft and unmanageable, rewrap it and refrigerate for 30 minutes. Arrange the palmiers flat on the prepared baking sheets, spacing them 2 inches (5 cm) apart. Sprinkle the remaining cheese mixture on top, along with any cheese that has fallen out.

✧ Bake until the cheese melts and the pastry is crisp and golden outside and fully cooked inside, 12–15 minutes. Transfer to a wire rack to cool. The palmiers will keep in an airtight container for up to 2 weeks.

Pecan Gift Bags

SUGAR AND SPICE PECANS • CELLOPHANE BAGS • RIBBON

1 Make the Sugar and Spice Pecans (page 87). Store the nuts in an airtight container until you are ready to make the gift bags for your guests.

2 One day before your party, assemble cellophane bags or other gift bags or small clear plastic boxes, as well as ribbon in various festive colors.

3 Fill each bag or other container with the nuts. Tie with a bow. If you like, attach a personal greeting or card with the recipe for the nuts. Place the bags in a basket or on a platter near the front door. Invite each guest to take one home.

Sugar and Spice Pecans

Simple to make, these pecans are at once subtly sweet and ever so slightly spicy. You can substitute another nut, or a mixture of nuts, for the pecans. They can be stored for at least 2 weeks.

4 cups (1 lb/500 g) pecan halves

2 teaspoons grapeseed or peanut oil

5 tablespoons (3½ oz/105 g) firmly packed turbinado sugar or brown sugar

1 teaspoon coarse salt

½ teaspoon ground cinnamon

¼ teaspoon ground cumin

¼ teaspoon ground allspice

¼ teaspoon cayenne pepper, or more to taste

MAKES 4 CUPS (1 LB/500 G) PECANS

✧ Preheat oven to 350°F (180°C). Spread the nuts on a rimmed baking sheet and toast, stirring once or twice, until lightly browned, about 10 minutes. Remove from oven and immediately transfer to a large plate.

✧ Heat a large, heavy frying pan over medium-high heat until very hot. Add the oil and nuts and stir to coat evenly. Sprinkle with the sugar, salt, cinnamon, cumin, allspice, and cayenne. Cook, stirring constantly, until the sugar melts over the nuts and caramelizes, about 2 minutes. (If the nuts start to burn, reduce the heat slightly.) Return the nuts to the rimmed baking sheet, spreading them evenly, and let cool.

Marinated Goat Cheese

This savory gift is a welcome departure from holiday confections. Attach a card on top with suggestions for serving, such as added to a green salad or spread on crostini, and include storage information.

✧ Have ready 1 hot, sterilized 1-pt (16–fl oz/ 500-ml) jar and its lid (see page 96).

✧ Put the cheese in the jar. Tuck in the bay leaves and sprinkle with the peppercorns, thyme, and rosemary.

✧ Pour the olive oil over the cheese in the jar, adding more if needed to cover the cheese completely. Wipe the rim and seal tightly with the lid.

✧ The cheese can be stored in the refrigerator for up to 1 month. Bring to room temperature before serving.

About 10 oz (315 g) firm fresh goat cheese, whole, sliced, or formed into small balls

2 bay leaves

12 peppercorns

1 teaspoon dried thyme

1 teaspoon dried rosemary

1 cup (8 fl oz/250 ml) extra-virgin olive oil

MAKES ONE 1-PINT (16–FL OZ/ 500-ML) JAR

Olives with Orange and Fennel

These flavorful olives make an unusual addition to any selection of hors d'oeuvres. For these and the olives on the opposite page, use an attractive glass jar, ceramic crock, or other container.

✧ Have ready 1 hot, sterilized 1-pt (16–fl oz/500-ml) jar and its lid (see page 96).

✧ Pat the olives dry with paper towels. Place on a firm work surface and, using the side of a large knife, crush each olive just until the skin cracks. Place the olives in the jar.

✧ Lightly crush the fennel seeds in a mortar with a pestle. Add the seeds to the olives, along with the orange zest strips and bay leaves. Pour in the olive oil, adding more if needed to cover the olives completely. Let stand for 4 hours at room temperature.

✧ Wipe the rim and seal tightly with the lid. Refrigerate for at least 2 days to allow the flavors to blend. The olives can be stored in the refrigerator for up to 2 months.

1½ cups (8 oz/250 g) brine-cured black olives such as Kalamata or Niçoise

1 teaspoon fennel seeds

3 orange zest strips, each 2 inches (5 cm) long by 1 inch (2.5 cm) wide

2 large bay leaves, preferably California

¾ cup (6 fl oz/180 ml) extra-virgin olive oil, or as needed

MAKES ONE 1-PT (16–FL OZ/500-ML) JAR

Lemon-Spice Olives

For a doubly welcome gift, give one crock filled with these green olives and another with the black olives on the facing page. Quality olives can be found at delicatessens and well-stocked food stores.

1½ cups (8 oz/250 g) large green olives such as French or Spanish

½ small lemon, thinly sliced crosswise

¾ cup (6 fl oz/180 ml) extra-virgin olive oil, or as needed

1 teaspoon dried oregano, crumbled

½ teaspoon red pepper flakes

½ teaspoon freshly ground black pepper

MAKES ONE 1-PT (16–FL OZ/ 500-ML) JAR

✧ Have ready 1 hot, sterilized 1-pt (16–fl oz/ 500-ml) jar and its lid (see page 96).

✧ Pat the olives dry with paper towels. Place on a firm work surface and, using the side of a large knife, crush each olive just until the skin cracks. Place the olives in the jar. Add the lemon slices.

✧ In a small saucepan over medium-low heat, combine the ¾ cup olive oil, oregano, red pepper flakes, and black pepper. Bring just to a simmer. Pour over the olives, adding more oil if needed to cover the olives completely. Let stand for 4 hours at room temperature.

✧ Wipe the rim and seal tightly with the lid. Refrigerate for at least 2 days to allow the flavors to blend. The olives can be stored in the refrigerator for up to 2 months.

Cheddar-Herb Shortbread

Enriched with both cheese and butter, the dough for these savory shortbread cookies is prepared in advance of baking. Even 24 hours of chilling allows the trio of fresh herbs to infuse the dough.

1 cup (8 oz/250 g) unsalted butter, at room temperature, cut into small cubes

1 cup (4 oz/125 g) finely shredded sharp Cheddar cheese

Leaves from 1 small bunch fresh thyme

Leaves from 1 small bunch fresh oregano

Leaves from 2 or 3 fresh rosemary sprigs

2 cups (10 oz/315 g) all-purpose (plain) flour

1 teaspoon sea salt, plus extra for garnish (optional)

MAKES ABOUT 5 DOZEN SHORTBREADS

✧ In a large bowl, combine the butter and cheese. On a cutting board, chop the thyme, oregano, and rosemary leaves as finely as possible. Add the herbs to the butter mixture and mash with a fork until evenly distributed.

✧ Add the flour and the 1 teaspoon salt. Mix first with the fork and then with your hands until the flour is incorporated.

✧ Divide the dough in half and quickly roll each portion into a log 8 inches (20 cm) long by 1½ inches (4 cm) in diameter. Wrap each log in plastic wrap and refrigerate for at least 24 hours or up to 3 days, or freeze for up to 1 week. (If frozen, thaw in the refrigerator for 24–36 hours before slicing.)

✧ Preheat oven to 350°F (180°C). Line 2 baking sheets with parchment (baking) paper. Cut each log into slices ¼ inch (6 mm) thick. Arrange the slices on the prepared baking sheets, spacing them about 1 inch (2 cm) apart.

✧ Bake until the edges begin to brown, 12–15 minutes. Remove from oven, sprinkle lightly with additional sea salt, if desired, and let cool for 2–3 minutes on the baking sheets. Transfer to wire racks to cool completely.

PRESERVED
DELIGHTS

Tangerine Curd

This rich, smooth curd is an ideal gift at Christmastime, when citrus is at its best. You can substitute tangelos, which are a cross between a mandarin and a grapefruit.

✧ In a small saucepan, bring the tangerine zest and juice and the lemon juice to a boil over high heat. Cook, stirring occasionally, until reduced to ¾ cup (6 fl oz/180 ml), about 20 minutes. Let cool.

✧ In a nonreactive heatproof bowl set over (not touching) simmering water, whisk together the whole eggs, egg yolks, and sugar until the mixture is thick and a pale lemon color, 6–7 minutes.

✧ Add the butter, 1 cube at a time, stirring until it has completely melted before adding the next cube. Add the reduced juice and zest mixture and whisk to combine. Cook, whisking, just until the mixture has thickened enough to coat the back of a spoon, about 3 minutes. Do not let the mixture boil.

✧ Have ready 3 hot, sterilized half-pint (8–fl oz/250-ml) jars and their lids (see right). Ladle the hot curd into the jars, filling to within ¼ inch (6 mm) of the rims. Wipe the rims clean and seal tightly with lids. Set aside to cool completely, about 30 minutes. The curd can be stored in the refrigerator for up to 2 weeks.

How to sterilize jars and lids *Sterilizing jars and lids is easy and helps safeguard against spoilage. Thoroughly wash the jars and their lids in hot, soapy water and rinse well. Place the jars upright in a large pot. Fill the pot with hot water, covering the jars by 1 inch (2.5 cm). Cover the pot, bring to a boil, and boil vigorously for 10 minutes at altitudes of 1,000 feet (305 m) or less; add an additional minute of boiling time for each 1,000 feet of elevation gain. Remove the pot from the heat and leave the jars in hot water until ready to use. Place the washed and rinsed lids in a small saucepan. Add water to cover, bring to a boil, and remove from the heat. Leave the lids in hot water until ready to use.*

Grated zest of 6 tangerines

3 cups (24 fl oz/750 ml) fresh tangerine juice

½ cup (4 fl oz/125 ml) fresh lemon juice

3 large whole eggs, plus 2 large egg yolks, at room temperature

½ cup (4 oz/125 g) sugar

⅔ cup (5 oz/155 g) unsalted butter, at room temperature, cut into ½-inch (12-mm) cubes

MAKES 3 HALF-PINT (8–FL OZ/ 250-ML) JARS

Preserved Lemons

In the Middle East and North Africa, preserved lemons are added to stews, salads, and other dishes. Meyer lemons, which are sweeter than other varieties, can also be used.

✧ Pour 3 qt (3 l) water into a nonreactive saucepan, place over high heat, and bring to a boil. Add the lemons, return to a boil, and cook for 3–4 minutes. Drain and immerse the lemons in cold water until they are cool enough to handle. Drain again.

✧ Have ready 2 hot, sterilized 1-qt (1-l) jars and their lids (see page 96). In a nonreactive saucepan, combine 6 cups (48 fl oz/1.5 l) water and the salt, cinnamon, coriander, peppercorns, cloves, and chile. Bring to a boil over high heat, then remove from the heat.

✧ Tightly pack the whole lemons into the sterilized jars. If you wish, you can halve or quarter the lemons lengthwise for a tighter fit. Ladle in the hot liquid, including the spices, to within 1½ inches (4 cm) of the jar rims. Add the olive oil to within ½ inch (12 mm) of the rims. Wipe the rims clean and seal tightly with lids. Let stand at room temperature until cool.

✧ To test the seal, press down on the center of a lid and then lift your finger. If the lid remains depressed, the seal is good. Store sealed jars in a cool, dark place for at least 2 months before using, to allow the lemons to take on the flavors of the brine. They will then keep for up to 6 months. If the seal has failed, store in the refrigerator for up to 3 months.

7–10 slightly underripe lemons, scrubbed

⅔ cup (5 oz/155 g) sea salt

2 cinnamon sticks

4 teaspoons coriander seeds

2 teaspoons peppercorns

8 whole cloves

1 dried chile such as New Mexico or Long Red

About 1 cup (8 fl oz/250 ml) extra-virgin olive oil

MAKES TWO 1-QT (1-L) JARS

Blood Orange Marmalade

Here, brilliantly hued blood oranges yield a jewel-toned marmalade for the holidays. The marmalade can also be made with navel oranges or, if you can find them, Seville oranges.

7 large blood oranges, scrubbed and quartered

2 lemons, scrubbed and quartered

7–8 cups (3½–4 lb/1.75–2 kg) sugar

MAKES FOUR 1-PT (16–FL OZ/ 500-ML) JARS

✧ Place the fruit in a nonreactive pot, add water, and let soak overnight. Remove the fruit and cut into slices about ⅛ inch (3 mm) thick. Return the fruit to the water, place the pot over high heat, and bring to a boil. Reduce the heat to medium-high and simmer uncovered, stirring occasionally, for 1 hour.

✧ Have ready 4 hot, sterilized 1-pt (16–fl oz/ 500-ml) jars and their lids (see page 96).

✧ Add the sugar to the fruit, stirring until dissolved. Clip a candy thermometer to the side of the pot and continue to boil until the thermometer reads 220°F (104°C), 20–40 minutes longer. After about 20 minutes, the color will deepen to amber, and as the temperature rises, the bubbles will become smaller.

✧ Ladle the marmalade into the jars, filling to within ¼ inch (6 mm) of the rims. Wipe the rims clean and seal tightly with lids.

✧ Place the jars, not touching, on a metal rack in a large pot, and add boiling water to cover by at least 1 inch (2.5 cm). Cover, return to a boil, and boil for 15 minutes.

✧ Using tongs, carefully remove the jars from the hot water bath and let stand until cool. To test the seal, press down on the center of a lid and then lift your finger. If the lid remains depressed, the seal is good. The sealed jars can be stored in a cool, dark place for up to 6 months. If a seal has failed, store the jar in the refrigerator for up to 2 weeks.

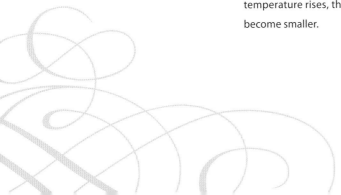

Cranberry Chutney

Ginger, citrus zest, and an array of spices flavor this aromatic chutney. When you dress up the jars as gifts, take the time to include the recipe and tips on serving—with ham, duck, cheeses, or pâté.

½ cup (4 fl oz/125 ml) cider vinegar

2 cups (14 oz/440 g) firmly packed brown sugar

3½ cups (14 oz/440 g) fresh cranberries

1 cup (4 oz/125 g) dried cranberries

1 cup (6 oz/185 g) golden raisins (sultanas)

¼ cup (1½ oz/45 g) crystallized ginger, chopped

2 tablespoons grated orange zest

1 cup (8 fl oz/250 ml) fresh orange juice

2 large Granny Smith apples, peeled, cored, and cut into ¼-inch (6-mm) cubes

1 tablespoon vanilla extract (essence)

2 teaspoons ground cinnamon

½ teaspoon ground cloves

½ teaspoon ground allspice

1 cup (4 oz/125 g) chopped walnuts, toasted

MAKES 6 HALF-PINT (8–FL OZ/ 250-ML) JARS

✧ Have ready 6 hot, sterilized half-pint (8–fl oz/250-ml) jars and their lids (see page 96).

✧ In a large nonreactive saucepan, combine the vinegar, brown sugar, and ½ cup (4 fl oz/ 125 ml) water. Bring to a boil over medium heat, stirring until the sugar is dissolved.

✧ Stir in the fresh and dried cranberries, raisins, ginger, orange zest and juice, apples, vanilla, cinnamon, cloves, and allspice. Bring to a boil and cook, stirring, until the fresh cranberries pop and the mixture thickens, 15–20 minutes. Remove from the heat and stir in the walnuts.

✧ Ladle the hot chutney into the jars, filling almost to the top. Wipe the rims clean and seal tightly with lids.

✧ Set aside to cool completely, about 30 minutes. The chutney can be stored in the refrigerator for up to 2 months.

Packaging Ideas

JARS, BOTTLES & TINS • RIBBON & TISSUE • GIFT TAGS

Preserved treats, both sweet and savory, are a welcome and lasting gift during the holidays and offer a great way to make use of seasonal ingredients.

Special bottles Package infused vinegars and oils in pretty bottles of unusual shapes. Adorn with ribbon, a gift tag, and a recipe for your favorite vinaigrette.

Sparkling glass Jams, jellies, chutneys, and other colorful preserves glisten like jewels when presented in jars, including round, squat glass containers.

Old-fashioned tin Line small tin buckets with tissue and/or cellophane for holding savory or sweet baked goods. Tuck in a gift card or tie on a recipe card.

Spicy Peach Jam

Cloves, cardamom, and cinnamon add an earthy spiciness to this luscious peach jam, which is delicious on buttered toast or biscuits. Prepare it during summer, the height of stone fruit season.

✧ Have ready a large bowl of cold water. Bring a large saucepan of water to a boil. Add half of the peaches and blanch for 30 seconds. Transfer the peaches to the bowl of water. Repeat with the remaining peaches. Drain the peaches, then peel, halve, and pit them. Working over a large, heavy nonreactive saucepan, slice the peaches lengthwise, allowing the slices and juices to fall into the pan. Stir in the sugar, lemon juice, cinnamon, cardamom, and cloves. Let stand for 1 hour.

✧ Have ready 2 hot, sterilized 1-pt (16–fl oz/ 500-ml) jars and their lids (see page 96).

✧ Place the pan over medium heat and cook, stirring, until the sugar dissolves. Clip a candy thermometer onto the side of the pan. Raise the heat and bring to a slow boil. Cook uncovered, stirring occasionally at first and then more frequently near the end of cooking, until the thermometer reads 220°F (104°C), about 30 minutes.

✧ Ladle the jam and even amounts of spices into the jars, filling to within ¼ inch (6 mm) of the rims. Wipe the rims clean and seal tightly with lids.

✧ Place the jars, not touching, on a metal rack in a pot and add boiling water to cover by 1 inch (2.5 cm). Cover, return to a boil, and boil for 15 minutes.

✧ Using tongs, carefully remove the jars from the hot water bath and let stand until cool. To test the seal, press down on the center of a lid and then lift your finger. If the lid remains depressed, the seal is good. The sealed jars can be stored in a cool, dark place for up to 6 months. If a seal has failed, store the jar in the refrigerator for up to 2 weeks.

---

8 peaches, about 4 lb (2 kg) total weight

4 cups (2 lb/1 kg) sugar

¼ cup (2 fl oz/60 ml) fresh lemon juice

2 cinnamon sticks, each 3 inches (7.5 cm) long

10 cardamom pods

4 whole cloves

MAKES TWO 1-PINT (16–FL OZ/ 500-ML) JARS

Plum-Vanilla Preserves

Allspice, cinnamon, vanilla, and citrus juices give these preserves an alluring depth of flavor. Plums are at their finest in midsummer, allowing you to make the preserves well in advance of the holidays.

10–12 plums, preferably purple-fleshed Santa Rosa, about 4 lb (2 kg) total weight

1 cup (8 fl oz/250 ml) fresh orange juice

½ cup (4 fl oz/125 ml) fresh lemon juice

4 whole allspice berries

2 cinnamon sticks, each about 3 inches (7.5 cm) long

7 cups (3½ lb/1.75 kg) sugar

1 vanilla bean, broken in half and then split lengthwise

MAKES FOUR 1-PT (16–FL OZ/ 500-ML) JARS

✧ Have ready 4 hot, sterilized 1-pt (16–fl oz/500-ml) jars and their lids (see page 96).

✧ Halve and pit the plums, then cut into slices ½ inch (12 mm) thick. Place in a large, heavy nonreactive saucepan and add the orange and lemon juices, allspice, and cinnamon. Bring to a boil over high heat. Reduce the heat, cover, and simmer, stirring occasionally, until the plums are very tender, about 20 minutes.

✧ Add the sugar and vanilla bean and stir until the sugar dissolves. Clip a candy thermometer onto the side of the pan. Simmer uncovered, stirring and crushing the fruit with the back of a wooden spoon occasionally at first and then more frequently near the end of cooking, until the thermometer reads 220°F (104°C), about 45 minutes.

✧ Ladle the preserves and 1 vanilla bean piece into each jar to within ¼ inch (6 mm) of the top. Wipe the rims clean and seal tightly with lids.

✧ Place the jars, not touching, on a metal rack in a pot and add boiling water to cover by 1 inch (2.5 cm). Cover, return to a boil, and boil for 15 minutes.

✧ Using tongs, carefully remove the jars from the hot water bath and let stand until cool. To test the seal, press down on the center of a lid and then lift your finger. If the lid remains depressed, the seal is good. The sealed jars can be stored in a cool, dark place for up to 6 months. If a seal has failed, store the jar in the refrigerator for up to 2 weeks.

Gingered Cranberry Relish

This versatile relish is made spicy with crystallized ginger. It is an excellent accompaniment to roasted chicken or turkey. The jars can be stored in the refrigerator for up to 2 weeks.

2 cups (8 oz/250 g) fresh cranberries

1 cup (8 oz/250 g) sugar

3 tablespoons minced crystallized ginger

MAKES TWO 1-PT (16–FL OZ/ 500-ML) JARS

✧ Have ready 2 hot, sterilized 1-pt (16–fl oz/ 500-ml) jars and their lids (see page 96).

✧ In a large saucepan, combine the cranberries, sugar, and ½ cup (4 fl oz/ 125 ml) water. Bring to a boil over medium-high heat. Reduce the heat to medium and cook, stirring often, until the juices have thickened and a few berries have begun to pop, 10–15 minutes. Stir in the ginger and remove from the heat.

✧ Ladle the hot cranberries into the jars, filling to within ¼ inch (6 mm) of the rims. Wipe the rims clean and seal tightly with lids. Set aside to cool completely.

Cherries and Prunes in Brandy

This is a great way to preserve summer cherries for holiday enjoyment. Both fruits make an elegant topping for vanilla ice cream or pound cake. See page 94 for a photo of the cherries.

Cherries in Brandy

1 lb (500 g) cherries, with stems intact

½ cup (4 oz/125 g) sugar

About 1 cup (8 fl oz/250 ml) brandy

MAKES ONE 1-PT
(16–FL OZ/500-ML) JAR

Prunes in Brandy

5 oz (155 g) large prunes

⅓ cup (3 oz/90 g) sugar

½ cinnamon stick

2 long strips orange zest

2 long strips lemon zest

About 1 cup (8 fl oz/250 ml) brandy

MAKES ONE 1-PT
(16–FL OZ/500-ML) JAR

Cherries in Brandy

✧ Have ready 1 hot, sterilized 1-pt (16–fl oz/500-ml) jar and its lid (see page 96).

✧ Trim the cherry stems to 1 inch (2.5 cm). Using a toothpick or thin bamboo skewer, prick each cherry 6 or 7 times. Pack the cherries into the jar. Sprinkle the sugar over the cherries. Pour in enough brandy to cover the fruit completely. Wipe the rim clean and seal tightly with the lid. Store in a cool, dark place for at least 3 months before using; the cherries will keep for up to 1 year.

Prunes in Brandy

✧ Have ready 1 hot, sterilized 1-pt (16–fl oz/500-ml) jar and its lid (see page 96).

✧ Pack the prunes into the jar. Sprinkle the sugar over the prunes. Tuck the cinnamon stick and strips of citrus zest down into the jar, keeping them next to the glass so they are visible. Pour in enough brandy to cover the fruit completely. Wipe the rim clean and seal tightly with the lid. Store in a cool, dark place for at least 3 months before using; the prunes will keep for up to 1 year.

Index

OXMOOR HOUSE

Oxmoor House books are distributed
by Time Inc. Home Entertainment
135 West 50th Street, New York, NY, 10020

VP and Associate Publisher Jim Childs
Director of Marketing Sydney Webber
Brand Manager Victoria Alfonso

CHRISTMAS GIFTS FROM THE KITCHEN

Conceived and produced by Weldon Owen Inc.
415 Jackson Street, San Francisco, CA 94111
Tel: 415-291-0100 Fax: 415-291-8841
www.weldonowen.com

A Weldon Owen Production
Copyright © 2009 Weldon Owen Inc.

Color separations by Mission Productions
Printed and Bound in China by SNP-Leefung
First printed in 2009
10 9 8 7 6 5 4 3 2 1

Library of Congress Cataloging-in-Publication
data is available.

ISBN-13: 978-0-8487-3295-0
ISBN-10: 0-8487-3295-2

WELDON OWEN INC.

CEO and President Terry Newell
Senior VP, International Sales Stuart Laurence
VP, Sales and New Business Development Amy Kaneko
Director of Finance Mark Perrigo

VP and Publisher Hannah Rahill
Associate Publisher Amy Marr
Assistant Editor Julia Nelson

VP and Creative Director Gaye Allen
Associate Creative Director Emma Boys
Designer Lauren Charles

Production Director Chris Hemesath
Production Manager Michelle Duggan
Color Manager Teri Bell

Group Publisher, Bonnier Publishing Group John Owen

Food Stylists Kevin Crafts and Jamie Kimm
Stylists Lauren Hunter and Sarah Slavin
Contributing Authors Georgeanne Brennan, Kerri Conan, Abigail Dodge,
Jean Galton, Shelly Kaldunski, Jeanne Thiel Kelley, Kristine Kidd, Lori
Longbotham, Ray Overton, Tina Salter, Michele Scicolone

All photography by Jim Franco except for the following: Emma Boys
(pages 76, 95, and 103 bottom); Aimée Herring (pages 46 top and
103 top); Keller & Keller (pages 2, 5, 6, 46 bottom, 65, 66, 70, 78–79, 89,
and 106); David Matheson (page 53); and Ellen Silverman (pages 40,
47, and 50).

Weldon Owen wishes to thank the following individuals for their
editorial assistance: Carrie Bradley, Ken DellaPenta, Judith Dunham,
and Peggy Fallon.